I CAN READ IT ALL BY MYSELF

Beginner Books

For Maria with love
—A. D.

Library of Congress Cataloging-in-Publication Data:

DeCesare, Angelo. Anthony the perfect monster / by Angelo DeCesare.
  p. cm.—(Beginner books)
SUMMARY: Anthony has always been perfect, but starting school makes him
feel like a perfect monster instead.
ISBN 0-679-86845-3 (trade) — ISBN 0-679-96845-8 (lib. bdg.)
[1. Perfection—Fiction. 2. Monsters—Fiction. 3. Schools—Fiction.] I. Title. II. Series.
PZ7.D3553An 1996 [E]—dc20 94-26105

Printed in the United States of America   10 9 8 7 6 5 4 3 2 1

ANTHONY
the Perfect
MONSTER

by Angelo DeCesare

BEGINNER BOOKS   A Division of Random House, Inc.

Everyone said
Anthony was perfect.

"Perfect," said his mother.

"Perfect," said his father.

"Perfect," said his baby-sitter.

"Purr-fect," said his cat.

But being perfect was hard.
Every day Anthony had to
comb his hair
and brush his teeth
and button all his buttons.
Then he had to be
nice and quiet and polite.
All the time.

Anthony was perfect
when his mother said,
"Wear your raincoat."
Even though it was sunny outside.

He was perfect when his father said,
"Eat your spinach."
Even though Anthony hated spinach.

He was perfect
when his baby-sitter said,
"Play quietly."
Even though Anthony
wanted to be loud.

But even perfect boys
have to go to school.
"I know you'll be perfect,"
his mother said.
"Yes, Mother," said Anthony.

On the first day of school,
Anthony combed his hair

and brushed
his teeth

and buttoned
all his buttons.

Then his mother
decided it was chilly outside.
So Anthony bundled up.
"Now everyone will see
how perfect I am!" he said.

But when Anthony got to school,
the other kids stared at him.

Some even pointed and whispered.

It made him feel shy.

But he tried to be perfect anyway.

He raised his hand
when the teacher
asked for a helper.
And he raised his hand
each time the teacher
asked a question.
"Please give the others
a chance, Anthony,"
said his teacher.

That day after school,
Anthony saw some boys
with Super Splurters.
Anthony stood between the boys.
"Let's play a nice game
like Tippy-Toe Tag," he said.

But the boys didn't listen.

Anthony walked home.

He had tried so hard to be perfect.

But no one seemed to like him.

No one even seemed to care.

That night,
Anthony's parents went out.
Anthony went to bed early.
But he couldn't sleep.

Anthony's baby-sitter
was watching a movie.
It was the kind of movie
Anthony never watched.

It was about a man named Harry.
Harry turned into
a horrible monster
whenever he hiccuped.
He was called Horrible Harry Hiccup.

Horrible Harry ran wild.
He growled and he howled.

OWOOOOOO

He jumped
on the bed
without taking off
his shoes.
Horrible Harry was not
perfect at all.

Anthony went back to bed.
And thought about
Horrible Harry Hiccup.

The next morning,
Anthony woke up tired and cranky.
He didn't comb his hair
or brush his teeth.
He didn't even button
all his buttons.

Then his mother said,
"Anthony, put on
your raincoat.
It's going to rain!"
But Anthony knew
it was a sunny day.
He didn't want
to wear his raincoat.
Anthony got mad.

"If I were a monster," said Anthony,
"I could do whatever I wanted to do!"
Anthony got madder. And madder.
"I wish I were a monster!" he said.
"I wish, I wish, I..."
Anthony hiccuped.

And it happened!

He let out a long, loud growl.
It sounded a lot like
"I don't want to wear it!"
Anthony ran past his mother.

Anthony raced down the street.

He saw the two Super Splurter boys.

They were playing Crasher Smashers.

"I want to play too!" roared Anthony.

"Sure!" said the boys.

They charged at him.

Anthony let out a growl!

He charged back.

Down they went with
a monster bump.

"Wow!" said the boys.

In school,
Anthony crouched on his seat.
Not once did he raise his paw
to be a helper
or give an answer.

Finally, the teacher asked,
"Anthony, do you know
the Spanish word for 'yes'?"
"Growr-rowr!" Anthony yelled.

All the kids laughed.
They laughed
and laughed
and laughed.

Anthony's feelings were so hurt
that he ran out the door.

Anthony hid in the hall closet.
Inside, he cried
as only a monster could.
A very sad monster.

A while later, his teacher
opened the closet door.
"Maybe I can help,"
she said kindly.
"I tried so hard to be
perfect," he said.
"But nobody likes me!"

Anthony's teacher smiled
and led him into the hall.
All his classmates were there—
cheering!

"But how can you all like me?"
Anthony asked.
"I said no to my mother.
I ran wild and played rough.
I cried and growled.
I acted just like a monster!"

"A monster?
You sound like
a normal kid to me!"
said Anthony's teacher.
"Nobody can be perfect,
no matter
how hard he tries.
It's a lot easier
to be yourself...
and a lot more fun!"

Anthony's mother
was waiting for him after school.
"Do you still love me?" he asked.
"Even though I'm not perfect?"
His mother smiled.
"Of course I do!" she said.
And she gave him a great big hug.

So that's how
Anthony stopped trying
to be the most perfect kid.
He became, instead, a kid
who was sometimes angry,

sometimes sad,

sometimes happy.

But always perfectly...himself!